Words From the Heart

By Lena Butterworth

Words From the Heart

Copyright © 1998

Lena Butterworth
First Printing 1998

Published by:
Lena Butterworth
P.O.Box 675
Mountain Home, AR 72654-0675

ISBN: 1-57502-973-1

Library of Congress Catalog Card Number: 98-93686

Printed in the USA By

MORRIS PUBLISHING

3212 E. Hwy 30
Kearney, NE 68847
800-650-7888
Fax: 308-237-0263

DEDICATION

*To my Lord, whose arms are always open
and stand ready to enfold me,
thank you for the gift of words.
To my devoted family
and to my endearing friends,
I extend my deepest gratitude
for your unwavering love,
encouragement and support.*

ACKNOWLEDGEMENTS

Every so often in your lifetime you encounter people who are extremely knowledgeable and who are willing to share their knowledge and expertise with you. And, they do it with smiles on their faces. Fortunately for me, such was the case with THAT PRINT SHOP in Mountain Home, Arkansas - my present home town. Without their guidance and ongoing support, the pursuit of the publication of my first book could very well have turned into a nightmare! Instead, it has been an enlightening and pleasant experience even though I burned the midnight oil on many evenings. I have many books on my shelves at home and I have read them and referred to them dozens of times. It simply amazes me that I never gave a single thought to the amount of preparation and hard work it must have taken to reach the end result. Well, now I know.

I would like to express my sincere appreciation to Denise, Randy, Gina and Carolyn - especially Carolyn, who was mainly responsible for the preparation of my book and for "putting it all together". I do thank each of you from the bottom of my heart.

Lena Butterworth

iii

TABLE OF CONTENTS

FAITH

Don't ever think for one minute -
even in your darkest hour -
that your faith has left you.
You may cover it up,
at times ignore it, misplace it -
perhaps even lose it for a while -
but it stands firm.
God is always at your door
waiting to bless you with peace of mind
and contentment.
All you have to do is let Him in!

SHADOWS AND RAINBOWS

Grant me your blessings and guide me, my Lord,
as you listen to my every prayer;
help me to feel your presence, Lord,
and to know you are always there.

Shadows and rainbows are both part of life
and I know days are touched by each;
hidden in shadows are dark stormy days,
yet a rainbow awaits within reach.

I pray you will show me a trouble-free place
where peace and contentment abide;
I know I can face every shadow each day
and touch rainbows with you at my side.

LOOK TO GOD

Somehow we seem to muddle through
all the unpleasantries of life;
those things which test our faith and courage
and fill up our days with strife.

Sometimes our minds get so confused
and we feel we are all alone;
we seem to forget that we possess
an inner faith all our own.

We may misplace it now and again
and forget to kneel and pray;
yet all we need do is follow the glow
of the bright light He shines our way.

So, whenever life's problems get you down,
just look to the heavens above;
and you will find strength and solace
in the power of God's divine love.

LORD, BLESS ME TODAY

Lord, give me courage that I may face
every trial I must meet today;
help me to know you are at my side
and to feel your presence, I pray.

Guide every step on a faithful path
as I follow your guiding light;
keep me safe from all harm, dear Lord,
from morning and into the night.

TROUBLE AND WOE

Troubles are a part of life
and you'd better believe I know it;
and when our woes pile one on one,
our temperaments will show it.

But, if we put our trust in God,
then He will hear us saying;
"Lord, 'til my troubles go away,
I'll just keep right on praying."

A DAILY PRAYER

Oh! Lord, I need your help today
to guide my tiny boat;
and so I humbly pray to you
to help me stay afloat.

The storms are many -
wild and fierce -
and as I muddle through;
I seem so overwhelmed sometimes
and so I turn to you.

I know you can see me,
I know you can hear me.
Please help me, please bless me
and walk with me today.

A LITTLE BIT OF FAITH IS ALL I NEED

If I have the tiniest bit of faith,
as small as a mustard seed;
then God will answer my humble prayer
and help me in my time of need.

I will sense His presence come over me
and feel the touch of His hand;
and for a while He will carry me,
and for a time I will look and see
one set of footprints in the sand.

And when my time of trouble has passed
and He's mended my broken wings;
then I will bravely fly once again
and give thanks to our King of Kings.

TRUST IN GOD

The roads of life are never paved
with easy paths, it's true;
and there may be some rainy days
along with skies of blue.

But when the trials that come your way
are more than you can stand;
just reach up to the sky above
and God will take your hand.

Then He will lead you day by day
to do the things you must,
if you will only look to Him
with faith...with love...and with trust.

I NEED THEE, LORD

Oh, Lord, I am lost - help me find my way.
Lord, I am weak - help me to be strong.
Lord, I am burdened - ease my heavy load.
Lord, I am so troubled - grant me inner peace.

GOD IS EVERYWHERE

God is in His heaven and watches over you,
but while He watches you every day,
His eye is on me, too.
God is in the mountains and high upon the hill,
beside the wild and stormy sea,
or by the water still.
God is in the valley and in the meadow, too,
and when you feel you need a friend,
He will comfort you.
God is all-forgiving and when you pray, you'll see.
The simple reason to it all?
He loves both you and me!

COPING

Some days may be dark days,
while other days are bright;
but when my days are stressful,
I pray with all my might...
that wherever my road leads me,
and no matter what I do;
that God in all His wisdom
will help to see me through.

AT LAST I CAN BE
"JUST ME!"

God gave me life on the day I was born
and He gave me a mind and a soul;
He said, "Child, go out and make your own way"
and He gently put me in control.

My growing-up years as they flash through my mind
show the reins were held tightly on me;
when my parents commanded, I strictly obeyed
and I was what they wanted me to be.

And then there were teachers one after another
and I did what they wanted me to do;
my mind and my body struggled each day,
yet somehow I managed to get through.

Then came the wedding, the honeymoon, too,
but no storybook marriage was there;
for soon all the pages were tattered and torn
and the chapters were filled with despair.

Then came another who entered my life
and days had their joys and their sorrows;
when God called him home I said, "What comes next?
What will happen with all my tomorrows?"

And when I decided to pose that question
to My Lord, My Saviour, My God -
He opened His arms and He held me tightly
and He gave me such a reassuring nod.

He said, "Child, I have been right here at your side
while you struggled, but now you have learned
that I want you to spend the rest of your life
leaving no stone in your pathway unturned."

So, now with high spirits like the eagles that fly,
I'm spreading my wings as wide as can be;
for of all things - right now - in my golden years -
I have the opportunity to be "Just Me!"

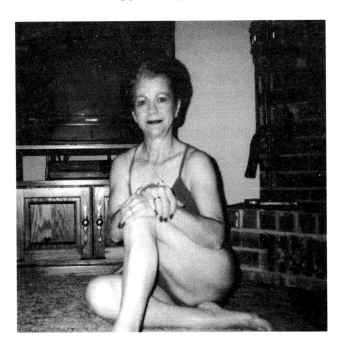

FAITH RENEWED

My Lord, I was as a fallen sparrow.
My body was filled with pain.
My thoughts were laced with bitterness and anger
and my heart ached for peace I could not find.

I wasted so many days reliving sorry yesterdays
and I faced the future with fear and uncertainty -
with much more doubt than I care to admit -
and with more mistrust than I have ever felt before.

It is difficult for me to understand
how it happened that I came to this road.
At what point did I take a wrong turn?
How could I have questioned your love for me?

What caused me to forget momentarily
that at any time in my life when I could not walk,
it was then that you carried me in your arms,
safe and secure until not only could I walk,
but I was able to fly once again!

Then came thy wondrous holy light!
A miraculous turnaround happened in my life!
Now I can soar like an eagle - arms outstretched
towards heaven reaching for thee.

I heartily regret having strayed from thee
and I know in my heart that during the moments
when I was lost, you kept a constant and watchful
eye on me and you alone renewed my faith.

I know that you are most merciful, Lord;
that you are kind and all-forgiving,
and that you do not punish your children
for their weaknesses of the mind and spirit.

Lord, please bless those whom I dearly love
and those who love me in return.
May they realize how special and precious
they are to me and let them know that
their love kept me from straying even further.

I pray for strength to face bravely
whatever each day holds in store for me.
Help me to remember that I am never alone.
Let me be ever aware of thy holy presence
and thy guiding and loving touch.

Please mend my body and bless me with good health.
Let my mind be ever thankful for thy constant love
and fill my heart with peace for the rest of my days.

I MUST BELIEVE

My Lord...

I do not presume to understand your ways;
I cannot comprehend your reasons;
I fail to see why illness strikes us down -
or horrible calamities occur -
or unexpected tragedies befall us -
or why temptation stalks us,
or why we succumb to it.

I cannot fathom reasons why
people can be so mean to each other,
spewing out vicious hateful words,
acting in animalistic ways
and cruelty unbecoming civility.

Though I have taught myself to accept,
surely you must realize my concern -
concern for those whom I love who falter
while waging a courageous daily battle;
compassion for those who suffer beyond tolerance;
and it is beyond my comprehension
why there are people who live in want
for just the bare necessities of life.

Yet I must believe in you,
for without you there is no hope -
without you life has no purpose -
and without you the salvation
of our souls would be impossible!

HOW MUCH TIME IS ENOUGH?

Once in a while when my thoughts get deep
and I think time is passing too fast;
or, on certain days when things go so right,
I keep praying, "Lord, please let this last."

There are times when I feel I would like to know
how much more time God will grant;
and each time I pray I feel like asking,
but somehow I know that I can't.

How many minutes will turn into hours
and how many days will I waste?
How many more times will I look back
at the trials and the troubles I've faced?

"What's done is done", I remind myself,
I should take life one day at a time;
for when I approach a mountain too high,
He gives me more strength for the climb.

There are so many things I have yet to give -
a kind word, a kind deed, or a smile;
for when you get down to the purpose of life,
these things are what make life worthwhile.

So whenever a feeling of doubt sets in
and my fear or anxiety mounts;
I know that it's not how much time He gives us,
it's what we do with it that counts.

WALK WITH ME, LORD

Lord, my mind is so confused,
somehow I've lost my way;
please let me feel thy presence, Lord,
as I humbly kneel to pray.
Please lead me to a quiet place
to ease my worried mind;
I know the peace I seek is there,
for He who seeks shall find.
There is no greater joy in life
than walking, Lord, with thee;
but when I stumble and I fall,
then, will you carry me?
I pray each day in time of need
when I have lost control;
that a heavenly light will soon appear
from thee, the Savior of my Soul.

LOVE

There may well be as many facets to love
as there are stars in the sky.
To name a few --
spiritual love,
parents for their children
and their children's children,
mother-son, father-daughter,
daughter-mother, son-father,
love of country,
love of peace and tranquility,
love of a good book or good food,
love of animals,
love of a trusted confidante
and, not at all in an egotistical way,
love of oneself.
Of course, the most wonderful love of all
is the love which you carry in your heart and share
with that very special companion in your life -
the single, most important person
who makes the journey
on this place we call earth
more special and magical
than you ever dreamed was possible.
What has been stated
a thousand times or more in the past
is indeed quite true:
"Love makes the world go 'round!"

WHEN I LOVE SOMEONE

You can brag about all of your conquests
all you care to.
Me? When I love, I'm a one-man woman
and I love with every breath I take,
with every fiber of my being,
with all my heart
and with all my soul.

The first kiss in the morning
is the sweetest.
The kisses during the day
are comforting.
Ah, but the kisses at night
are so passionate
that they can send my blood
racing though my veins.

"Me, me, me" doesn't exist.
Everything in life is "us" and "we".
Time spent apart is sometimes pure torture,
but time spent together is always precious.
Just to be able to love and be loved
helps to make life's most difficult times
so much easier to bear.

Sharing your silliest notions,
your innermost thoughts
and your wildest hopes and dreams,
provides the much-needed support
for a rich, fulfilling life.
Some women call me crazy
when I say
that the sun rises and sets
on the man I love.
His happiness and comfort
is what I live for.
But then, that's me!

TALK TO ME

Please don't sit there quietly
for, dearest one, you see;
it is your sweet and soothing voice
that calms and comforts me.

I need for you to often say
how much I mean to you;
and have you hold me in your arms
when each busy day is through.

So, come and sit beside me, love,
and tell me about your day;
and I will snuggle close to you
to hear what you have to say.

You know how much I love you
in a hundred different ways;
and you're the only one who brings
bright sunshine to all of my days.

THE MAGIC OF LOVE

Isn't it something? -
    that you can change my mood
    from bad to good.

Isn't it ironic? -
    that once I thought it difficult
    to be with someone
    day after day after day -
    now I'm certain
    I wouldn't like living alone.

Isn't it magical? -
    that when I am cross
    one word or one look from you
    transforms me
    into a gentle being.

Isn't life wonderful?

Isn't love grand!

THOUGHTS OF YOU

I thought of you today, as I did yesterday.
Locked safely in time are sweet memories of you.
Secreted in my heart are all the happy moments
    I cherish of our lives together.

I thought of you this morning...
    as I walked to the mailbox
    hoping to find a letter from you -
    and I smiled because there was.

I thought of you this evening...
    as I watched the sunset flood the sky
    with shades of yellow, orange and red.

As I turned down my bed at the end of the day,
    then nestled between the sheets,
    I wondered how many times
    I had thought of you today...

I thought of you today...
    more than yesterday...
        but less than I will tomorrow.

NOW THAT I'VE FOUND LOVE

Now that I've found love,
I know the joy of closeness.
I know that each day brings us nearer
heart to heart.

Since I've known your touch,
I carry it with me everywhere I go
from morning to night
day by day.

If my day goes right
you are there to listen
to the inconsequentials
that filled my hours.

When everything goes wrong,
you offer your shoulder,
or your hankie,
or your unwavering support,
or all of the above.

When I am with you,
I am proud of you
and the way you look.

In a crowded room a glance reaffirms
that we belong to one another -
not in a sense of ownership,
but in a sense of sharing,
caring and loving.

Now that I've found love,
there are no limits to my success,
no boundaries to my dreams
and no end to my devotion,
now that I've found you.

WHO GETS THE KITCHEN TONIGHT?

When vows were exchanged on the day we were wed,
I was not suspect of my doom;
but now in my mind's eye an apron I see
being worn 'round the waist of my groom.

If only he'd given a hint or fair warning
when he proposed down on his knee;
he should have confessed of his secret desire
to try every known recipe.

At first I rejected infringement upon
my humble and rightful domain;
I later relented - for no fool was I -
but my friends said, "You must be insane!"

"A man in the kitchen will bring sure disaster,
he'll leave pots and pans everywhere;
the scene will resemble a cyclone that hit,
so remember our words and beware."

Well, they were all wrong and I'd like to tell them
what a super whiz he has become;
as he bustles around our country-style kitchen,
I can hear his soft confident hum.

Though I'm quite adept at cooking and baking
and my specialties make quite a list;
our children would phone and honestly state
that Dad's was the cooking they missed.

So here's to you, Love, may I offer a toast -
you're fantastic with a capital "F" -
and I can say proudly, without reservation,
"My man's not a cook, he's a Chef!"

My dear departed husband simply adored it
when I wrote a poem especially for him.

Here's one...

HAPPY ANNIVERSARY, HONEY!

I think of all the years we've shared
together you and I;
my heart is filled with happiness
and you know the reason why.

For you have given so much joy
and purpose to my life;
there's nothing else I'd rather be
than your sweet adoring wife.

I composed this poem in 1985
The Lord called Bill home in 1995

MY HUSBAND, BILL

When I am lost and can't find myself,
you are there to help me look;
and when I feel I don't know myself,
you can read me like a book.

When I am down and feeling blue,
you bring a smile to my face;
we share so many sweet memories
that time could never erase.

For God heard my prayer so long ago
and answered from high above;
I knew I was the luckiest one
when he sent me you to love.

My husband, my lover, my best friend -
all these things are you to me;
as we go through life - my hand in yours -
and into eternity.

To My Husband: My Valentine

Valentine, Oh, Valentine!
You ask me the question,
"Will you be my Valentine?"
Yet, I am sure you know the answer.

I have been your Valentine
    for so many years.

We have come so far through
    mopping feverish brows of children,
    waiting in hospital corridors,
    stopped-up drains,
    missing trains,
    running out of gas
     on a desolate highway
     (<u>after</u> we were married!).

Somehow we survived through
    accolades and barbs,
    raises and cutbacks,
    promotions and demotions.

But we have reveled together in
picnic-in-the-park celebrations,
dancing at Willowbrook Ballroom,
the glow of the fireplace,
the tenderness of our hands touching,
countless romantic evenings
(and mornings).

You have always been there
through my numerous hospital stays
bearing flowers and gifts,
supporting my endeavors,
giving me wise counsel,
listening to bad-day reports,
through moments of tears and sorrow,
intermingled with endless hours of joy.

So, ask me the question that you,
my truly devoted, ever-faithful
and dependable Capricorn,
ask of me every year,
"Will you be my Valentine?"

And I will answer as I always do,
since it is only you I love,
"I will be your Valentine -
today -
tomorrow -
and forever after."

TIME FOR US

Many years ago life meant
    flowers and candy, courting, getting engaged,
    planning a wedding, whispering "I Do" at the
    altar, sealing our vows with a kiss and
    looking forward to more time together.

As the years went by it was
    singing lullabies to sleepy-eyed children,
    changing diapers, taking temperatures, nursing
    sick children back to health, and adjusting to
    the newness of parenting - there was no time
    for "us".

Before we knew it time came for
    the first day of school, the first visit from
    the Tooth Fairy, witnessing the winner of the
    class spelling bee (Is that really "our" child
    up there?), and graduation - we treasured
    occasional moments together.

With disbelieving eyes we saw
    a young freshman begin high school with
    trepidation, a know-it-all sophomore emerge,
    a junior setting new track records, and
    (proudly) the valedictorian of the senior
    class at graduation - the "time for us" was
    getting closer.

From college came short notes
"Don't change my room", My funds are getting
low", "Sorry I missed your birthday, Mom, I
was cramming for exams", and "May I bring a
friend home with me for the holidays?"

Lately the rooms of this house faintly echo with
sibling rivalry, incredibly loud stereos,
pillow fights, pajama parties, constant chatter,
and the laughter of young voices. Suddenly
the silence was deafening.

Do you detect sadness? I guess only a little.
But with indelible paint from the brush of time,
the memories are treasured separately and
yet intermingled with one another.

So! "Now" is a "time for us". And what a time
we are having!

A WEDDING

Here comes the bride, a pure vision is she,
in her gown trimmed in beading and lace;
he stands in his tux looking nervous and pale,
but with such a proud look on his face.

Now there's a hush and in a velvety voice
she, in sweet pledge of love, says "I Do";
he holds her hand as he whispers the same
and he vows all her dreams will come true.

Blessings upon them for now they are wed,
in the eyes of our Lord it is done;
they entered the church as separate people,
then two separate people became one.

Two hearts are joined now in one loving heartbeat
and we wish them a long happy life;
for no greater joy can be found here on earth
than the joy of a husband and wife.

MY LIFETIME VALENTINE

Dear Valentine, I love you
for all the countless ways,
your love brings joy into my life
and brightens all my days

I treasure every moment
and nothing can replace,
my happiness when I can see
a smile upon your face.

I need no worldly fortunes,
no matter what their worth,
because two hearts that share a love
is the richest thing on earth.

You know I'll always love you
and want you to be mine;
there's no one else I'd rather have
for my lifetime Valentine

LOVE IS GRAND ... OR, IS IT?

There was a nice fellow named Harry,
who searched for a girl he could marry;
but it drove him insane,
for his search was in vain
and he thought he'd commit hari-kari.

There was a nice man name of Frankie,
who met a sweet thing tall and lanky;
but she was a sensation,
had a bad reputation,
for what you might call hanky-panky.

Now this is the story of Randy
who thought that his girlfriend was dandy;
but she had roving eyes,
flirted with other guys,
so, Randy stopped sending her candy...
and flowers...and jewelry...
well, you get the picture!

There was a nice fellow named Chuckie,
when you see him he acts very plucky;
his head's in a whirl,
'cause he found the right girl
and he knows that he's really quite lucky.

34

There was a short lady named Shirley,
who smiled with such teeth white and pearly;
but, the fellows saw through her,
oh, yes, they all knew her
to be a mean bossy old girlie.

A fellow named Jack was so lonely,
he longed for his true one and only;
but, elusive was she,
so, dejected was he;
ah, love is a bunch of baloney!

There once was a cutie called Grace,
who searched for a man every place;
but, try as she might,
every beau was a fright,
so, she finally gave up the chase.

ABOUT LOVE

Don't allow yourself
to go on a frenetic search for love.
Just wait ... it will come to you
when you least expect it.
Say to yourself,
"The harder I try,
the more I fail;
sometimes I cry,
but Love will prevail."

NO TIME TO TALK

Sometimes I feel so sad and blue
and I think I know what's the matter;
I think it's because you don't have the time
to listen to my silly chatter.

So in order to clear my cluttered mind
I have an idea that's better;
I'll sit myself down with pen in hand
and write you a newsy letter.

There are so many things I want to share
'cause you know that I love you to death;
but if I waited 'til you found the time,
I'd turn blue just holding my breath!

THINKING OF YOU

As I go about my daily routine
it's amazing how often I find,
that in the course of my busy day
thoughts of you enter my mind.

And so I'd like to tell you now
just how much I really love you,
and there isn't an hour that passes by
when I'm not thinking of you.

Whenever we seem to be out of touch
and even though we're far apart,
just remember how often I think of you
and that I love you with all of my heart.

BILL - A HERO

When America was called to war,
you answered your country's call;
and you bravely faced our enemies
to preserve freedom for one and all.

You and thousands just like you
were ready right from the start;
you left your loved ones far behind,
but you kept them in your heart.

And as you marched off to dangerous places,
not knowing what was in store;
you faced the challenges proudly
as so many had done before.

You wondered if we thought of you,
but you were happy to learn;
we blessed your names, put stars in our windows
and prayed for your safe return.

Not one of us could ever imagine
the horrors that you would face;
and many unlucky ones never came home -
they died in some faraway place.

Yes, you watched your comrades die
before your very eyes;
while ships were tossed like toys afloat
and thunder filled the skies.

A soldier pledges his life to preserve
our honored red, white and blue;
so, with our gratitude, love and respect -
we will always remember you.

Written: May 23, 1995
Dedicated: May 24, 1995

TO BILL: A FOND GOODBYE

Remember when you asked me to
promise to pursue my writing of poetry
and composition of music and that I did so without
hesitation? It was an easy promise to make because
I knew that I would not and could not ever break
that promise. In my heart, I feel that you are
proud of my accomplishments.

Here is something which I wrote for you
on August 7, 1995, just a few months
after you left us ...

I cannot see you face to face,
or hold you close to me;
for now you sleep in peace, my love,
and Angels sing to thee.
Yet every day I think of you
and every day I pray,
that God will keep you in his care
and I'll see you again some day.

With Love,

Lena

LET TIME STAND STILL

I have the power within myself
to freeze a moment in my mind;
and so I store it carefully
for one day I know I will find,
that I will want to recall it at will
from a cherished place and then;
I can relive it at quiet times
again and again and again.

And this is what I do with each
of the precious moments we share;
for even though we are miles apart,
it seems like I'm standing right there.
So if at times when we are together,
it appears that my mind goes astray;
it's just because I'm capturing moments
to treasure another day.

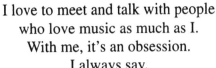

I LOVE MUSIC

I love to meet and talk with people
who love music as much as I.
With me, it's an obsession.
I always say,
"A day without music
is like a day without sunshine."
The stereo plays music
as soon as I have
one foot out of bed.
I may still be trying to wake up
as I sip my morning coffee...
but I can still hum to the radio.
When I get into my car,
I turn on the ignition and next,
a tape is inserted into the tape player -
it's automatic!
Be it songs from the
Big Band era, Four Play,
a George Benson smoothie,
country and western,
or semi-classical music,
I love it all!

MOMMY, WHERE IS DADDY?

Child: Mommy, where is Daddy?

Mommy: He's sleeping, dear.

Child: Why don't I ever see Daddy when I get up in the morning? The bedroom door is always closed.

Mommy: It's because he's worked so many hours and he needs to get some rest.

Child: I know, but I wish he could have breakfast with us sometimes.

Mommy: He will, dear.

Child: When?

Mommy: I don't know the answer to that, honey. Well have to wait and see.

Child: You work, too, Mommy, but at least you're here most of the time.

Mommy: Well, my schedule is different from Daddy's.

Child: Why can't he have a ... a ... whatever you said ... like yours?

Mommy: His job is different. He has more responsibility.

Child: What does that mean?

Mommy: He just has more important things to do and people to answer to.

Child: Oh. Well, I wish I could climb up on his knee and get a great big hug from him right now, Mommy.

Mommy: Maybe you can do that when Daddy gets up.

Child: But I'll be in school, Mommy, and Daddy will leave for work before I get home. Then what? Will he tuck me in bed, tonight?

Mommy: I think you will be fast asleep before Daddy gets home, sweetheart.

Two weeks have gone by ...

Child: Where is Daddy, Mommy? I haven't seen him for so many days.

Mommy: Well, uh, ummm ...

Child: Mommy, what's wrong? Why are you crying? Where is Daddy?

Mommy: Honey, Daddy died a week ago. I just didn't know how to tell you.

 43

Say these words often to someone special in your life ...

I love you.

When I hold you, I hold a bit of heaven in my arms.

I love it when I can make you laugh.

It makes me feel so wonderful when you need me.

You put a song in my heart!

No matter the weather, we'll always be together.

You are the most precious thing in my life.

Your smile can brighten any moment.

Talk to me. I love the sound of your voice.

I miss you whenever we're apart.

You have the most gentle touch I have ever known.

I'm ecstatic when I hear you say, "Hi, Honey, I'm Home".

FAMILY

Isn't family life the greatest? Being a member of a family
makes one a very significant part of something that is
the very core of the American way of life. What's nice and
special about it, too, is that there's always "someone" to
do "something" with. Okay, so having the measles at
the same time as my sister, Luci, and brother, Kelly,
isn't exactly what I had in mind. Mother certainly had her
hands full at that time, but she was the strongest and
yet gentlest person I have ever known. I miss her every
day. Daddy was a hard worker and, to my recollection,
missed going to work only one day his whole life.
Steadfast and true - that was my Daddy!

This was a letter which I mailed
to members of my family and to a few close friends
on January 3, 1997.

It referred to the photograph below which I took of
myself on New Year's Eve, December 31, 1996.

Every time I look at the picture behind me, I
think of myself as the former "fallen flower". (See
it to the right of my head in the photo?) But even
though I have fallen a number of times, you have
always been there to pick me up and put me back
into the "bouquet of life". For that you have my
everlasting love and gratitude.

If we are to learn anything at all from what we experience in our daily lives, then I think it is this -

Pray for good health because without it, everything else is meaningless.

Treat your loved ones as precious jewels. Love them with all your heart and tell them and show them that you love them.

Be grateful for all the good things in your life and do your best in coping with the worst.

Speak kindly to friends, neighbors - and at times even strangers - for they may be your best allies.

Do not be a taker. Instead, be a giver - and do so with a smile and a happy heart.

Always remember that what goes around comes around and you reap what you sow. Do not be dishonest, disloyal, mistrusting, offensive, mean, aggressive, or vindictive.

I love you and you are always in my thoughts and daily prayers.

REFLECTIONS OF MY LIFE
July 2, 1997

Driving home from town today I began to think about the years I have spent enjoying country living. "Far cry from city living", I said aloud. As I traveled the narrow road that would take me home, the sun blinked through the trees in the forest. Then suddenly a strange feeling came over me. I took a deep breath in an attempt to inhale the beauty of it all and store it deep inside me. I knew in my heart that this time in my life was coming to a close. In contrast to the indescribable beauty of trees on acres and acres of land in a dot-to-dot-like fashion, bluffs reaching high into the heavens, animals of every species imaginable wandering about day and night, the world-renowned White River and our beautiful twin lakes, I can still envision my tired body trudging along with hundreds of others and making my way to the law office where I spent the last 12 years of my secretarial career. It seemed that we were in our own little world in the famous "Chicago Loop". Although I don't regret the experience I gained and the sense of fulfillment of an exciting career, I don't miss it one iota. I closed that chapter of my life when I retired.

There is something justifiably comforting about a normal schedule or routine. It gives one a sense of continuity in one's life. But, now I ache for the unknown excitement of the future. I want to be kept so busy that I don't even have time to think! Lately I have been consumed with the fear of not having enough time left to do what I want to do with the rest of my life. My mind continually races a mile a minute and every thought is filled with plans, hopes and dreams. I pray every day that the Lord will guide me and shower His blessings upon me and allow me to experience the realization of some of them.

It is often said, "Be careful what you wish for ... you just might get it!" Well, my dreams are "nice" dreams. And my goals will never hurt anyone -- at least I hope not! I may step "over" a few people along the way, but it will never be my intention to step "on" anyone to reach them. So, while I have given the lazy and quiet life a big chunk of my life and I can mutter, "been there, done that", it is time for me to move on.

When the time comes to close a chapter in our lives, we tend to do so with a tinge of sadness. Although there is nothing wrong with hanging on to memories of the past, we must not live in it. The days ahead may range from bright and sunny to dark and stormy. It will undoubtedly be a mixture of the two. But when God closes a door, He opens a window. As I contemplate closing a chapter in my life, I look forward with great anticipation to what the future may hold. As long as I put my faith and trust in God, keep a smile on my face, give thanks for the good things in my life while doing my best in coping with the worst, I will face the dark shadowy days that test my tenacity as best I can until the sun breaks through once again. I shall always remember every day that God is with me. He may allow me to falter now and then, but He will always be there to pick me up, or to carry me, if necessary. He would never allow me to fail as long as I continue to believe in Him. Why? Because He loves me! I will close these reflections of my life with the inspiring words from Corinthians 13:7-8 ... Love knows no limit to its endurance, no end to its trust. Love still stands when all else has fallen.

49

THOUGHTS OF THE PAST
July 9, 1997

When I look at this photograph of myself in my high school graduation cap and gown, my mind is flooded with memories. Oh, it was such a long time ago! And yet, sometimes it seems like it was only yesterday that I was standing in front of our home in the city of Chicago. Mom was insisting I pose this way and that saying, "Now, put your hand up to your graduation cap." Or, "Let's take one of you standing on the front steps."

My parents were Italian immigrants. Their main concern was to put food on the table for themselves and their young ones. Their days were long and tedious. Mom labored in the fields like so many other women in Italy. When the time came for women to give birth to a child, they went off to a secluded spot, gave birth, and then went right back to work. There was no doctor, no nurse and no hospital. A midwife took care of everything. As a young boy Daddy walked miles and miles from his home to a nearby farm - sometimes in the snow - with no coat to keep his body protected from the elements and no shoes on his feet. He labored all day long, was fed, then walked his way back home to get some sleep. That was his young life.

Guts, courage, stamina, strength, endurance - give it any definition you choose - they just don't make them like that anymore. My parents were not educated people, but they had more common sense than anyone. You couldn't pull the wool over their eyes - ever! And we found out early on that you couldn't get away with anything.

The most important thing I can remember about my childhood is that I always knew where I stood with Mom and Daddy. There was never any wishy-washy parenting; no "you-can-get-away-with-that-today-but-don't-try-to-get-away-with-it-tomorrow" episodes. They both passed away a long time ago, but often when something happens in my life that makes me happy or proud of myself, I find myself thinking, "How about that, Daddy?" Or, when I find myself slouching I think, "Mom, I can just hear you reminding me to stand up straight and tall." You both taught me so much about being a proud American, keeping the faith and never compromising my morals and principles.

Believing in my principles cost me the business award at graduation. The award consisted of an engraved plaque, which I would have cherished, and a brand new typewriter, which I certainly could have used. My teacher had already told me weeks before that the award for being the best typist in my senior class was deservedly mine. But, when she took me aside shortly before graduation day and instructed me to lie for her so that she could save face with school officials, I refused. She threatened to give the award to another student if I did not do this for her. Sobeit! Again I refused. When another student's name was announced on graduation day my Mom, my sister, Luci, and I choked back our tears. We knew in our hearts that I should have been the one walking to the podium to receive that award. But, they were proud of me and I was very proud of myself for sticking to my principles. See, Mom and Daddy? You taught me well. Thank you!

 51

THOUGHTS OF THE PAST
July 13, 1997

It is said that you can tell a lot by looking into someone's eyes. In fact, eyes have been referred to as "windows of the soul". I believe they are a true reflection of who you are and I think they are the most important feature on one's face.

Eyes can convey a heartful of love or affection, pride, hate, disgust, amazement - the list goes on. It bothers me when people don't look at you when they speak to you. They seem to be unable to devote their full attention to a conversation. Their eyes are constantly glancing to the left, to the right, or up or down. I would not like to have so cluttered a mind. I prefer looking at someone when I am speaking to them, because then I can get the full benefit of the emotions that come from within them which are created by the words I am saying to them.

In this photograph, I think my eyes say it all. They are clear, shining, happy and anticipating the future with excitement. I worked my little heart out to get a good education and when I graduated I felt that I had succeeded.

I was very proud of my accomplishments and I was fully prepared to give my best to every opportunity that would come my way. Only God knew what the future held for me. But, I always believed that every hour of every day would be precious for as long as I lived. They say that if you had all the money in the world you could not buy an extra 24 hours. So, I was going to cherish all the days of my life and make the most of them.

Mom always cautioned me to be "a good girl". And I was. Not only because she asked me to - I did it for myself. I heard too many stories from my senior classmates about their wild weekends. I never made any comments against their chosen lifestyle because God does not put us on this earth to judge others. I actually pitied them because surely they must have had a low esteem of themselves. What were they trying to prove? I have no clue. Not one of them was a good student. They didn't come to school to try to learn anything! School was a place where they came primarily to pass the time of day and to socialize. I often wonder where they are today.

The years have flown by too quickly since graduation. There have been times of great joy and times of deep sorrow in my life. Miraculously, my feelings of decency and fairness, sincere concern for others and compassion for their trials and tribulations and, most importantly, love of God, family and country have never left me. I am truly grateful to my parents for all the sacrifices they made so that they could provide a better life for their children than the lives they had. But they need never to have been ashamed of anything. Not once did they fail to give us the most important thing one can give to another - LOVE! Thanks, Mom & Daddy, for everything. Miss You - Love You!

53

MY FAMILY

If all the children in the world
were lined up side by side;
I would pick out Sue and Steven
and point to them with pride.

The problems that we face at times
may bring a tear or two;
but every day I love them more
no matter what they do.

It takes a lot of common sense
and a great deal of devotion;
a will of iron and nerves of steel
to withstand all their commotion.

Guiding, helping, at their side
is where I long to be;
there never will be words to tell
how much they mean to me.

A TRIBUTE TO MY MOTHER

From sunny Italy
she came
leaving a life
of hardship
and despair.

With hopes and dreams
of a better life
and small children
huddled
at her knees.

Warm thoughts of her
brighten my days
for sweet memories
are never
out of mind.

If it were not for her
I would not be...
my children and grandchildren
would not be
sparkling jewels in my life.

I can no longer touch her
yet she is not gone
and I love no other
like my Mother
and I know I never will.

BANANA CURLS

When my sister, Luci, and I
were innocent little girls,
our Mother would wrap
our long brown hair
into banana curls.
First, she took a clean white sheet
and ripped it piece by piece,
then as she combed she waited for
the tears we shed to cease.
With every tug and every pull
to smooth out every knot,
we asked her for
a more gentle hand
because we cried - a lot!
But when at last our hair was dry
and she combed it out for us,
we looked so downright beautiful,
she forgave us for all the fuss!

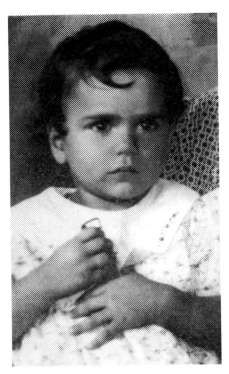

MY MOTHER

I wish I had my Mother near
with her endearing charms,
so she could gently cradle me
within her loving arms.

She gave me life - she gave me love -
each need did she fulfill;
and I will keep her in my heart
'til my time on earth stands still.

To my dear daughter, Sue...

By what stroke of luck did I become your Mother and you my daughter? From the time of conception I carried you with joy. After your birth when the nurse placed your rosy-pink loveliness in my arms, I was overwhelmed. With my very first look at you I envisioned your first birthday party, the terrible two's (and three's); and pictured you dashing off to school. I remember I was given the morning off so that I could take you to school on your very first day. But you walked a half-block ahead of me all the way to show your independence. Such a big girl! I guess I was proud and hurt at the same time.

So many years have gone by like a flash. Now, you have two daughters of your own. You have experienced first-hand both the joy and sadness of parenting. Mothers don't mind putting their wants and needs on the back burner for a while. I did it for you and now you do it for your own children. But, you can see the countless rewards, can't you?

You have filled my heart with pride on many occasions just when I thought the bottom was falling out of my world and all was lost. Troubled times were indeed a part of our lives but somehow, through the Grace of God, I remember only the good times and happy moments we have shared.

You know that I love you, but I wanted to tell you again. And I will keep telling you again ... and again ... and again.

All my love always,

Mom

To my dear son, Steve...

By what stroke of luck did I become your Mother and you my son? You were feisty from the day you were born. You really came into the world kicking! Little did I know when I looked into your big brown eyes the very first time that they would be my downfall for years to come. When you were naughty in school, your teachers would say that they could never really get angry with you when you gave them that look. As your Mother I came to know "that look" very well. But, even when it was necessary for me to visit your school and I was told of your mischief, I also could never get angry with you. I just chalked it up to your being your own person and not ever accepting any put-downs from anyone. If you were wrong, you were the first to admit it. But, if you were right, I was always proud that you were able to stand up for yourself.

Days, months and years have flown by as though they had wings. In a tiny corner of my mind, I can still envision my tired body aching from a hard workday and you standing behind the arm of the sofa in readiness to brush my long hair. You will never know how soothing that was. We've laughed together and many times you have given me your shoulder to cry on. No matter what hardships God placed in our path of life, being survivors we made it through.

You know that I love you, but I wanted to tell you again. And I will keep telling you again ... and again ... and again.

All my love always,

MY DAUGHTER, SUE

Some mothers have daughters
who don't seem to care;
they go separate ways
with so little to share.

They miss all the closeness
and that's really sad;
they long for affection
that they've never had.

That's why I'm so happy
we care as we do;
and I wish every mother
had a daughter like you.

A SPECIAL HUG JUST FOR SUE

One hug for you to be used as you need it,
no matter the time - day or night;
one loving hug to be ever repeated
to make all that's wrong seem all right.

One hug for you to be ever replenished,
it always will be there for you;
use it whenever you feel you need huggin',
or if you find you're feeling blue.

Use it when you are delighted and happy,
or when you have something to share;
just close your eyes and you will discover
the hug you need soon will be there.

Since I cannot be there whenever you need me,
there's only one thing left to do;
and that is to send to you one special hug,
it's a special hug just for Sue!

Written for my son, Steve - March 19, 1987

TRUCKIN'

I got the pedal to the metal
and the board to the floor
and I'm headin' for the open road.
I got my rig nice and shiny
and it sparkles in the sun
and I'm singin' as I'm truckin' my load.

My load can be some lumber,
or some pipe, or even steel,
it really makes no difference to me.
Just load me up and wave goodbye
and I'll be on my way,
for the road is where I want to be.

I go to Oklahoma, Texas,
Illinois or Kansas City,
and I travel to the north, south, east or west.
I feel a breeze through the window,
see the beauty of the country -
hey - this truckin' life is really the best!

I talk to other truckers
on my C-B radio
just to take up the long day's slack.
My C-B handle's "farm boy" - say,
"Have you got your ears on?
If you got a copy, come-on back!"

I'm gonna keep on truckin'
for a very long time,
so, believe what I'm sayin' is true.
I've got my Steve's Cartage jacket
and my Peterbilt truck
and, Lord, I sure love what I do!

Thank you, Lord...
for letting me be a trucker!

KELLY: A MASTER MUSICIAN

His Italian features were striking.
He fit the description: tall, dark and handsome.
Well, not unusually tall, but tall enough.
He had beautiful brown eyes,
sensuous eyebrows,
a smile that would melt any female heart
and "magic fingers" that would literally fly
across his accordion keys.
My favorite song that he played?
Tico Tico!
Somehow Daddy managed to find the money
for Kelly to have accordion lessons.
But, Kelly didn't stop there.
He also taught himself to play
a number of other musical instruments
and went on to become a music teacher,
a songwriter and a music publisher.
He and his trio performed at some
fabulous Chicago hotspots.
I used to love it when the guys
came to our house and Kel would
ask me to sing a tune they were practicing.
He used to say I sounded like Doris Day.
What a compliment!
He was a wonderful brother and an
extremely gifted musician.
I say "was" because as I write this,
he is most likely tapping a baton at
the podium in Heaven
and leading the Angel Chorus.
I miss you, Kel.

Here are two poems written for my sister,
Luci, through the years.

TO LU, WITH LOVE

Two sisters know a special love
that each has for the other;
bound by years of memories
they share with one another.
They walk a lifetime hand in hand
through childhood days so treasured;
the deep devotion that they feel
cannot be bought or measured.
A lasting friendship, tried and true,
no one on earth can sever;
and, Sis, the love I have for you
will last forever and ever.

TO MY SPECIAL SIS

You seem to always be the one
to show you understand;
you put a troubled mind at ease
and lend a helping hand.
In time of need you never fail
to unselfishly impart
a loving deed, a caring word,
that comes straight from the heart.
So, when you reach out lovingly
to someone young or old;
may every kindness that you do
return a hundredfold!

64

MOTHER'S DAY - May 11, 1986

To Granddaughters Chris & Stacey

The Grandmother card you sent to me
was lovely beyond compare;
I thank you for your thoughtfulness
in showing how much you care.

I've known such joy these passing years
that was multiplied by two;
I tried to help your dreams along
and was thrilled when some came true.

I've read your card so many times
and every time I do;
your faces are clear before me
and your love comes shining through.

It pleases me to do the things
that your card suggests I do;
but, it's easy when a Grandma has
granddaughters as special as you!

With Love,

Gram

CHRIS GOES TO COLLEGE!

Written for
Granddaughter Chris
August 13, 1989

Oh! it seems such a short time
when memories I tap,
since my Sue placed a grandchild
in my anxious lap.
I have such fond memories
of Chris in her youth;
her first words -- her first steps --
her very first tooth.
While in grade school she blossomed,
then high school was here;
graduation - elation -
we stood up to cheer!
While she garnered achievements
from first day to last,
we savored sweet moments
with each year that passed.
She's flown the coop now,
yes, she's left the nest;
she's gone off to college,
if you haven't guessed.
Time passes so quickly -
the years are a blur;
now, she's going to college -
we're all proud of her!

To Chris with much love...

Gram

SCHOOL IS OUT!

Written for Granddaughter Stacey,
when she was 11 years old.

Hip! Hip! Hooray!
Today's my last day
and now I'm already for fun;
I can ride on my bike,
or take a long hike,
or, just sit quietly in the sun.

Ring-a-ding-ding!
I feel I could sing
at the top of my voice loud and clear;
I could sleep until eight
or, go to bed late,
now that summer vacation is here.

School is okay,
but just let me say
I leave with a certain elation;
So, pardon my dust,
as hurry I must,
for a date with my summer vacation!

With Love,

Gram

Written for Granddaughter, Christine
and newly acquired Grandson, Jay T
on their Wedding Day
June 6, 1998

GOD BLESS YOU
ON YOUR WEDDING DAY

As you begin your married life together,
may the arms of love forever keep you warm;
may God protect you in all kinds of weather
and give you strength
to face your every storm.

If you can keep the love you share afire
and celebrate each day the Lord may give;
then He will grant your every heart's desire -
that is my wish for you
for as long as you both shall live.

With Love,

Gram

I composed this poem for my son and my daughter
just before I went to sleep on May 8, 1994.
To this day I have kept the sweet memories
of this lovely day in my mind and in my heart.

MY SPECIAL MOTHER'S DAY

It's getting quite late and I should go to bed,
but visions of lobster still dance in my head;
the steak was delicious - the wine, oh! so sweet,
and Steve made a salad that just couldn't be beat!

And Sue was there, too, with a kind helping hand,
oh! such sweetness and love only Moms understand;
this evening was special - thanks, Sue and Steve;
we had such great fun - why, I hated to leave!

So, when I recall the events of this day,
you'll know loving thoughts will be coming your way;
I'll send you my love on the wings of a star,
yes, this day was special -
because that's what you are!

With Love,

Mom

To My Daughter Sue
and My Son Steve

WHEN YOU REMEMBER ME

After I'm gone, whenever you remember me,
I would hope that the first and foremost thought
that comes into your mind
is how deeply I loved you.
It wasn't always easy, was it?
We came to an impasse quite often
about a number of things.
Even now when memories stir up the past,
it disturbs me that I couldn't always
get my point across as to why
I wanted you to do something or,
conversely, why I didn't want
you to do something.
Okay, so I didn't win all the battles,
but at least I didn't lose the war.
I suppose on occasion
we didn't even like each other.
Thank God true love runs deep
because no matter what happened,
the special bond between us
has always remained intact.
You have brought more joy
into my life than I ever
could have imagined possible.
It makes me so proud
to have you call me
Mother.

FRIENDS

One of the greatest blessings in life
is a good friend.
If you have one good friend
in your lifetime, you are fortunate.
But, if you have more than one,
consider yourself
truly blessed.
A true-blue friend accepts you
for who you are
and what you are...
no holds barred...
and no questions asked.
A good friend stands ready
to listen, but not criticize...
to advise, but not demean...
to help, but not judge...
and, above all, to offer encouragement
to see you through troubled times.
We should always be grateful
for good friends.

TO ANTHONY
FRIENDS FOREVER

A best friend is truly one of
life's greatest treasures;
they will always know exactly
how you feel.

There are no thoughts you cannot
share with one another,
and there are never any feelings
you have to conceal.

You can always tell a friend about
your cares and worries,
and without fail they will be there
to wipe away the tears.

But the nicest thing about a
special lasting friendship,
is that it becomes more beautiful
and stronger through the years.

And so my heart is ever grateful,
because I know all these things are true;
and every day I thank every star in heaven
for the wonderful best friend
I have found in you!

With Love,

Lena

73

Composed for My Best Friend
Anthony Toti
August 3, 1996
Alaska Bear Trip - August 17-24, 1996

WHO'S CHASING WHO?

I'll be leaving this town
in a couple of weeks
and soon I'll be chasing bear;
I can picture it now ...
it's so clear in my mind ...
it's like I was already there.

The excitement I feel
is so hard to describe
and I can't wait to start the chase;
yes, some of my friends say,
"You gotta be nuts"...
but I'm going in any case.

And once I am there
I don't know what I'll find,
I'll just have to wait and see;
my birthday just happens
to be that week
and there might be a trophy
waiting somewhere for me.

So, I'll tell you about it
when vacation is over,
I know I'll be glad I went;
and when all of you see
the bear I bring home,
you'll say,
"It was a week well spent!"

TO ANTHONY
MY SPECIAL FRIEND

A friend is one who shares your life,
in thought they're always near;
their warmth and charm and cheerful smile
make troubles disappear.

They have a way of bringing joy
into a trying day;
they care enough to somehow know
exactly what to say.

I'm sure you know I'm grateful for
the kind things that you do;
and I'm so glad that God gave me
a special friend like you!

With Love,

Lena

TO ANTHONY

HAPPY BIRTHDAY, DEAR FRIEND

A candle will be burning
on your special day this year,
because it's time to celebrate
now that your birthday's here.
Then as the candle slowly burns,
the glow that fills the room
will lighten up my lonely heart
and lift each trace of gloom.
Although I cannot hear the voice
that always makes my day,
or look upon your handsome face
because you're far away,
I'll hang this birthday wish for you
on every shining star
and somehow it will find you, dear,
no matter where you are.

With Love,

Lena

August 20, 1998

THE DAILY STRUGGLE

I worship him from afar.
That's the way it has to be.
We rarely have time to talk.
I am so disheartened. Too many
precious moments are slipping away
and they can never be recaptured.
He's entirely too busy...
so many problems... so many burdens...
so much responsibility.
Why does life have to be so tough?
He works so hard...
gives it all he's got and then some.
Talk about "beyond the call of duty"!
He doesn't smile much... too bad...
he has such a nice smile! But, no time to smile.
Not much time to laugh, either.
I often ask, "What can I do to help you?"
He looks at me and says, "Nothing!"
But he knows I'm here if he needs me.
For now I can only say, "Take care because
I love you and I worry about you so much."

You know what I think?
I think life is like a boxing match.
We put on our gloves every day
and we enter the ring.
We stand in our corner ready to fight!
In the opposite corner is the challenger
weighing in at 100 times our size.
We take a few steps forward and then
the blows begin... a jab to the left...
a jab to the right... an uppercut to the chin...
and the worst blow of all... a powerful punch
below the belt! That really hurts! What should we
do? Fight back, that's what! Strike a counter-punch
again and again - harder this time, until we knock the
opponent down and he can't get up!
We stand there triumphant!
Yes! Victory in all its splendor!
We feel a sense of relief and we relax.
But not for long... because when the battles of
today are over, suddenly we realize that we have
to do this all over again tomorrow!

FRIENDS

Friends are very special people
and they care with such devotion;
you can share with them your hopes and dreams
and every imaginable emotion.

Their love and guidance leads you through
by all they say and all they do;
I bless the day you came along -
what a wonderful friend I have in you!

THANK YOU FRIENDS!

I have read your kind words over
at least a dozen times or more;
and each time that I do
it touches my heart
more than the time before.

And in days to come be certain
I'll keep thoughts of you in my mind;
for I know I have found
the dearest of friends
that I ever could hope to find!

For Joan -

Life is full of ups and downs
with surprises by the score;
we never know from day to day
just what may be in store.

And though our spirits may be low,
why just around the bend
lies one of life's most precious gifts -
a special new-found friend.

A FRIEND IS A TREASURE

It's nice to know
that someone cares
and often thinks about you,
and tells you
just how sad and blue
their life would be without you.

For there's no greater
joy in life
when you come to
each day's end,
than knowing
just how lucky you are
to have such
a wonderful friend!

DEAR RED -

It's amazing how someone can enter your
life and make such a difference.
You certainly have made a big difference
in my life and it's pure pleasure to know you,
you big hunk!

Happy Birthday to You!

DEAR RED -

Sometimes a man will go to great lengths
to get extra attention, it's true;
but you have exceeded all bounds, kind sir,
with all this excitement over you!

Men keep things a secret and I'm not sure why,
as they continue to get sicker and sicker;
they don't realize that compassion and love
can help them heal that much quicker!

Be that as it may we have come to a road
which will test our true faith and endurance;
but you will remain in our hearts and our prayers,
on that you have every assurance.

TO MY FRIEND, PAT PRESTON

Have I ever told you in so many words
what your friendship has meant to me?
For who would have thought our paths would cross
and how lucky we both would be?

It just goes to prove as we struggle each day
to contend with our daily strife;
that just around the corner waits someone
who suddenly brightens your life.

That "someone" is special and always true-blue,
so willing to show that they care;
and when you need someone to help see you through,
it seems somehow they're always there.

And so in the friendship department, my friend,
take the biggest and well-deserved bow;
because if I have not told you before,
my dear, I am telling you now.

I'm so glad you're my friend!

TO JEAN AND EARL

A friend is someone dear to you,
a fond treasure, to be sure;
a bond is there to build upon
and through time it will endure.

A friend is there in time of need,
or to pass the time of day;
friends are so kind and wonderful
in all they do and say.

A friend accepts you any day,
at your worst or at your best;
and if you have one, say a prayer,
for you are truly blessed.

But when the friends are like you two,
what joy a friendship brings;
I had to let you know, dear friends,
that you are all of these things.

May God bless you both!

TO MY FRIEND "PAT" PHILLIPS

Some years ago my husband talked
of a "cream puff" I should meet;
he called her this because she was
so lovely and so sweet.

He talked about her winning ways,
her charm, her warmth and grace;
and I looked forward to meeting her
and seeing her face to face.

The day came when we finally met
and what my husband had said was true;
for all things that are good in life
are all wrapped up in you.

I'll always treasure my time with you
and sweet memories nice to recall;
for of all the gifts that God can give,
friendship is the best of all!

TO HUIE AND MONA

A Happy Anniversary Toast
October 27, 1996

Here's to a wonderful couple
and the many years they have shared;
and here's a cheer
for the friends who came
to show them how much they cared.

Let's wish them more years together
and bright sunny days ahead;
and won't they be glad
when we've all gone home,
they'll probably have one foot in bed!

I THINK OF YOU OFTEN

When I get lonesome
and I'm feeling blue,
do you know what I do?
I think about you!

I think of your kindness
and all the while,
I picture your face
and the warmth of your smile.

I think of the hugs
so sweet and sincere;
I remember the giggles,
the laughs and good cheer.

Yes, I think of you often
and want you to know,
the thought of your friendship
embraces me so.
I miss you!

Me ... lounging around with "Teddy".

My Mother & Father

Son Steve & I

88

Brothers Angelo & Kelly, brothers-in-law Bob & Ralph.

Susan & Steven, ages 4 & 2

Sisters Elvira & Luci

Steve & Sue

Son Steve & I clowning around.

Son Steve & I love to pose for
what we call our "lap photo."

College Graduate Chris with proud Gram

Granddaughter Stacey & I.

Sister Luci & I.

My sister Luci -
Vocalist & Composer

My brother Kel & I -
we were blessed with a special closeness.

 93

Me ... ready for the
promises of tomorrow.

One of my favorite photos with
my daughter Sue. She <u>was</u> a
lovely child and <u>is</u> a beautiful
woman.

Standing: Sister Olimpia, brother Angelo, Mom.
Kneeling: Sister Luci, brother Kel, then me.

Bill was so proud of his hole-in-one and rightfully so!

Son Steve with Stacy (left) & Chris (right).

Brother Kelly in his studio.

My brother Kelly

My sister Olimpia
& her husband Ralph.

HAIKU POETRY

If you are familiar with Haiku poetry
(pronounced "Hi-Koo"), then you know that
it is an unrhymed Japanese verse form
of three lines containing
5, 7 and 5
syllables, respectively.

By the old farmhouse,
I will secretly meet you.
Be still anxious heart.

Old stationery
and unsharpened pencils sit.
Write to someone soon.

When rearing children
you learn a lot and yet you
never learn enough.

What a rainy day!
Caught off guard, my Monday wash
plays charades outside.

Cloud so puffy white,
pick me up when you pass by;
find me a rainbow.

Sudden spring shower;
fresh, cool; my umbrella is
home in my closet.

Ozark mountaintops,
lost in the fog of morning
and out of my sight.

Arise, sleepy sun!
Warm and brighten my day and
see to the flowers.

Poor tired old road,
cracked and worn from travelers,
but you take me home.

Tulips in a row,
like little children standing
single file in school.

A defiant stance,
she tosses her curly head
as she tells me, "No!"

She climbs on my knee,
digs her elbow in my side
while getting settled.

A hunter's shot rings,
piercing the quiet morning;
duck for his dinner!

❖

Pheasant hiding in
tall grass thinking no one sees;
pheasant under glass!

❖

Ride in the country;
behold farmland, endless skies.
Be closer to God.

❖

You who cry out "wolf":
better be careful or the
wolf will devour you.

❖

Maples, Ash and Birch,
standing tall together like
one big family.

❖

Into the world, child,
no road leading anywhere
and pave your own way.

Darkness comes and stays
endless hours; suddenly all
aglow with fireflies.

Pole in the river,
sit and daydream; but, wake up!
The fish took your bait!

She cannot speak words,
just gurgles and coos sweetly,
yet I understand.

Oh, my little child,
tugging the hem of my dress
and my heartstrings, too.

What shall I do with
this day the Lord has given me?
Precious! Don't waste it!

My love, you are home,
done with restless wandering;
stay locked in my arms.

Steeple bell ringing,
welcoming all worshippers
and beckoning sinners.

❖

I know I'm lazy,
but let me sit and watch the
crazy world go by.

❖

My son, growing tall;
was your mother fast asleep
while you became man?

❖

Daughter, curls and lace;
my heart wrapped 'round her finger
and she won't let go.

❖

Oh, my cherished friend,
why can't you accept my faults
and let me be me?

People in church, hushed;
straining to listen to the
whispered words, "I do."

Highway traffic jammed;
inching and creeping like tons
of cold robot steel.

Hot pavement under
my soles; feels like lit candles
and tiny needles.

Shimmering river,
beautiful and treacherous;
where are you going?

THE COMPUTER AGE

When I decided to buy a computer a few years ago,
I thought to myself: "Piece of Cake!"
I figured it would be so much fun!
I could browse...
gather a wealth of information...
store my poetry and music...
send and receive e-mail...
design personal greeting cards...
play some games
and have a ball!
Little did I know I would be entering
a maddening zone of some sort.
In the beginning,
I was frustrated and I was intimidated...
I was confused and I was stymied.
There I sat...
a reasonably intelligent woman
who suddenly felt quite the opposite.
How does a computer
make you feel so stupid sometimes?
Who knows?
Well, I finally overcame the frustration,
confusion and feeling of stupidity
and my computer and I
are now getting along just fine,
thank you!
In fact, now you could say
we're buddies!

MONSTER BABY

Yes, I have entered "computer world"
and it's a world of a different kind;
there are so many things to open and close,
it sometimes boggles the mind.

I literally want to give it a "boot"
when it doesn't want to behave;
when I'm stuck in a program, I lose control
and I sit there and rant and rave.

I've heard that computer nerds give theirs a name,
but I simply do not want to hear it;
you'd be awfully surprised at the names I call mine
whenever I'm anywhere near it!

Though I may be frustrated
I really don't mind it;
there's a world in there somewhere,
I just have to find it!

MY ULTIMATE TREASURE
a/k/a "Mut"

I used to call you "Monster Baby",
but I promise you - nevermore;
for now I have much more confidence
than I have ever had before.

Each day I'd start at an early hour
and I'd sit there far into the night;
but "Confused" became my middle name
and I couldn't do anything right.

When people said, "There's a world in there,"
I found out they were not kidding;
I have so much power in my hands
and you quickly respond to my bidding.

Here's how we play the game ...
I open - you open
I save - you save
You do nothing - I swear!
I type - you print
I close - you close
you sound bells - when I err!

Yes, slowly but surely we have become friends
and you've given me hours of pleasure;
now I suppose I'll have to re-name you
and so, I'll call you "My Ultimate Treasure"!

SCHOOL DAYS
COMPUTER DAZE

It used to be reading, 'riting and 'rithmetic
years ago when we went to school;
we did the right thing,
we were really good kids
and we lived by the Golden Rule.

But today it's a whole different world, of course,
as computers have come to be
a big part of our life
causing more stress and strife,
they make us feel just like a fool.

In these modern times it just makes good sense
to seize every advantage we can;
for computers do offer
a sizeable coffer
of every subject that's known to man.

And so I forge on - so desperate am I
to conquer this monster machine;
it drives me to drink
and sometimes I think
"I can't do it" - but really I know I can.

And so things have changed - for the better I hope -
while I sputter and utter "Oh, shoot!"
Yes, gone are those days,
for today it's the craze
of "RAM" and "ROM" and "Reboot"!

108

MASTERING A COMPUTER!

Computers create a tension so thick,
you could cut it with a knife;
I have never felt more stupid, you know,
at any other time in my life!

Learning to run a computer, I found,
is tougher than I guessed it would be;
but I'll persevere and I'll figure it out,
it will never get the best of me!

LAS VEGAS

Is there any place in the world
as exciting and glamorous
as Las Vegas?
I don't think so!
Besides the unsurpassed beauty
of the glittering lights,
which is a given,
no matter what your interests are,
you can appease your appetite
for all of them in Las Vegas!
Fantastic food at a great price?
You bet!
Shows with gorgeous people
in exotic costumes?
Feast your eyes!
Famous entertainers?
Just pick your favorite and enjoy!
Movie theaters, museums,
fantastic bands ...
they are part of Las Vegas, too.
Then, of course, there's gambling.
Step up, folks, and try your luck!
A few coins ... one pull ...
well, you never know!

"THE ORLEANS" IN LAS VEGAS

There's a place I love in Vegas
and "The Orleans" is its name;
and if you never feast your eyes,
you have no one else to blame.

It's like a wonderland of sorts,
there's always lots to do;
and they make you feel so special
by the kind things that they do.

It seems each time I go there,
what a thrill I feel inside;
all at once my heart is filled
with emotions I can't hide.

And when it's time for me to leave,
I'm sad and torn apart;
but I shall keep sweet memories
of "The Orleans" in my heart!

THE COURTYARD CAFE
"THE ORLEANS"
LAS VEGAS

When I awakened from my slumber
a delight my eyes did see;
why, scrambled eggs and sausages
were beckoning to me.

So, I dressed myself in record time,
flew down the hall and BAM!
Then I said to waitress Linda,
"Got your message - here I am!"

Me ... with friends Elizabeth & Frank.

YOU ARE ALL VERY SPECIAL!

There's a hotel in Vegas called "The Orleans"
and it's really a sight to behold;
and in this hotel is a place called "Vito's"
and it's wonderful - so I had been told.
And so I decided to try it one night,
while thinking, "Oh, what can I lose?"
And when they presented the menu to me,
gosh, I didn't know just what to choose!

But aside from the fact the menu was great,
the service was beyond belief;
for no matter which server I had each time,
I whispered a sigh of relief!
It's a pleasure to dine where the service excels
and the staff is so pleasant to you;
and though they are always bustling about,
they take time for a smile or two.

Too soon it was time for my visit to end
and I realized the worst of my fears;
"Don't fall apart", I thought to myself,
but I fought hard to hold back the tears.
You know I will keep you in my daily prayers
and I surely will write now and then;
in the meantime I'll say, "Take care of yourselves
until we all meet once again."

Written for the Wonderful Vito's Staff
June 11, 1997

WHERE ARE THE PEOPLE?

The hustle and bustle of restaurant life
is a hectic one, to be sure;
it presents such frustration, tension and stress
and it seems that there is no cure!

The kitchen is ready, the chef is prepared
and the servers are all ready, too;
they have tried to anticipate every demand,
there is nothing more for them to do!

The place settings are lovely, shiny and bright,
complete with a fresh coffee cup,
and they would do handsprings
with thankful elation
if the diners would only show up!

WHAT PHIL SABOL WOULD SAY ABOUT FOOD

I've traveled far and wide, you know,
I've been to many places;
and in my travels I have seen
so many different faces.

But, what interested me the most, I guess,
was the kinds of food to savor;
some were as good as mother made,
yet some seemed to lack in flavor.

I've had vittles, steak and seafood, too,
and as I ate my waistline grew;
food was my weakness - well, bless my soul!
When you give me food, I lose control!

Do I eat to live, or live to eat?
That's really what perplexes;
but tell me, please, why did I eat
an armadillo in Amarillo, Texas?

WELCOME MR. JUAN ORTIZ

Welcome to Vito's - we're so glad you're here
and we wish you the very best;
we're sure that you know
every ounce of your patience
will surely be put to the test!

When diners arrive to appease their hunger,
just put on your happiest face;
and sooner or later
a calm will prevail
as everything falls into place!

You could sail the seas for days on end
and dock at a hundred ports;
but you'll never find
anyone to compare
to the people of Coast Resorts!

Written For Irvin Putt
June 22, 1997

THE GAMBLING DILEMMA

There's a lot to be said for the luck of the draw
and I'm finding that this is so true;
it's a matter of choosing the perfect machine
that will do what I want it to do!

I'm praying out loud, "Give me four of a kind"
and I wish it would answer my plea;
and when they appear I thank it profusely
and say, "I'm as thrilled as can be!"

Then again the high point of gambling you see
is getting a straight royal flush;
and when my eyes behold such a sight,
I scream - I holler - I gush!

But when I'm losing I'm down in the dumps
and I whisper, "Ain't no future in it";
and I remember the words that someone once said:
there's a sucker born every darned minute!

BLACKJACK

Blackjack is such a fascinating game,
but it can drive you up the wall;
you think you've got it all figured out,
but you don't have it figured out at all.

It seems at times you do everything wrong
and it makes you so mad you could spit;
you take a card, you bust and then say,
"Oh, why did I take that hit?"

Ah, yes, it's a game of luck I know
and most times it's downright cruel;
but you must follow the method of play
and adhere to each blackjack rule.

And though I am frustrated time and again,
I still manage to have some fun;
and it's quite a challenge for me to play
the game they call "Twenty-One"!

LEAVING "THE ORLEANS" OF LAS VEGAS

As the plane headed upward high into the sky,
I thought to myself, "Gee, how lucky am I!"
Now, why do I call myself lucky, you ask?
It's because in the glow of affection I bask!

I think of my friends scattered through Coast Resorts,
such wonderful people, all kinds and all sorts;
whenever I visit, they're all overly nice,
they treat me so well, I should thank them all twice.

From the time I arrive to the day I depart,
the kindness they show me goes straight to my heart;
the smiles and the kisses, the hugs they bestow
are signs of affection from those I love so.

But back to the plane, we are climbing once more
and I feel the same sadness that I've felt before;
and then all once I sighed and I smiled
until my eyes glanced at a mother with child.

You guessed it, the mother sat right next to me
and I thought to myself, "This just cannot be!"
For rest I had none on the eve that just passed
and I had looked forward to sleeping at last.

Yet sleep was elusive and I needed it so,
but babies do cry and wouldn't you know
her shrills, her cries and her sobs pierced the air;
no, I could not sleep - did she even care?

"She's too little", I said, as I heard her Dad curse,
then all of a sudden things got even worse;
she stood up, spit up, poked her Mom in the eye,
I tried to stay calm -- I really did try.

I was just about ready to admit my defeat,
then an angel appeared: "May I change your seat?"
I couldn't believe it, but I didn't care,
I gathered my "stuff" and I followed her there.

Not one seat, but two did she offer me now!
Was I a happy traveler? You bet! And how!
Yes, babies are sweet and babies are fine,
still I can't help saying, "I'm glad they're not mine!"

To the PBX Operators at The Barbary Coast
September 29, 1996

PEOPLE BEYOND 'XPECTATION!

Down "in the dungeon" there's a room with no view
away from the crowd up above;
and there sits a group of the nicest ladies
that you simply just have to love!

I've talked to them all in the past but now,
it's been my good fortune to meet
the voices I've heard many times before
that sounded so bright and so sweet!

Each one is "Miss Personality Plus"
and their expertise really amazes me;
with fingers so quick, minds sharp as a tack,
their knowledge delights and dazes me!

The affection I have for each of these gals
has been nurtured right from the start;
and there always will be a special place
for each of them in my heart!

Love you all!

Lena

To the PBX Operators at The Barbary Coast
October 2, 1996

FRIENDS ARE A BLESSING
FROM ABOVE

Every so often one enters your life
that you are so grateful you met;
they leave such a mark
with their kindness to you
that you never will ever forget.

They go out of their way to do such nice things,
they can't seem to do enough;
and when you're together
you soon realize
they are made of all the right stuff.

You can laugh together or cry together,
you can joke or even tease;
and if you are lucky
to have friends like this,
you had better get down on your knees

So this little poem is for all of you
for I feel I've been truly blessed;
I hope each of you knows
this comes straight from the heart,
I mean it - you're simply the best!

Lena

To The Gifted Performers/Musicians of "DEJA BLUES"
The Orleans Hotel & Casino
Las Vegas, Nevada
February 20, 1997

TO CORK, EDDIE, DICK, CHARLIE & TOMMY

There's a band that plays at "The Orleans"!
Man! Oh! Man! They are really great!
And when they start that downbeat,
well say, I can hardly wait!

They play so many familiar tunes
and you are free to hum along;
and sure enough they're bound to play
your all-time favorite song.

So, if you haven't heard them yet,
I'm here to spread the news;
you're in for a special treat, my friends,
when you listen to "Deja Blues"!

SILLY STUFF

One of these days,
perhaps in time for my next book,
I am going to write
more "silly stuff".
It's fun and besides, I like to think
that somehow, somewhere
I have made someone
laugh, giggle, or smile.
After all, they say it takes
72 muscles to frown and
only 14 to smile.
Just think of all the wrinkles
I will be preventing!

IT'S ALL BEHIND ME NOW

I cannot believe that my underwear size
went from five, to six, then seven;
as years went by my dress size increased
from seven, to nine, then eleven.

I now can recall what my doctor said
as I'd snicker and wince and scoff;
"You had better be careful 'cause after forty
the poundage just won't come off."

Ignoring his words, I just forged ahead
eating ice cream and candy and such;
the skirt that would not slide past my hips
proved I was eating too much.

But french fries with steak tasted awfully good
and whipped topping on my dessert;
and I'd tell myself without any remorse
"Now, really, so what can it hurt?"

Now buttons won't button and zippers won't zip
so, I guess it's high time to admit;
because I was constantly stuffing myself
my favorite garments don't fit.

So then I decided that I'd buckle down
and worked hard to flatten my tummy;
yes, alas and alack, I had to give up
every goodie that tasted so yummy.

So, go ahead, ask me just how I feel,
do I miss my treats? Boy, and how!
But, I look in the mirror and say to myself,
"It's all behind me now!"

SHOPPING WITH MOM

I can recall when I got the urge
to go on a shopping spree;
and so I said to sweet daughter, Sue,
"Would you like to accompany me?"

So, off we went with purses in hand -
off to the big city mall;
we laughed so hard at the clothes I tried on -
too big, too tight, too small!

Ah, yes, those were our fun-filled days
when we went from store to store;
but it was time we spent together,
who could ever ask for more?

Each time I came out of the fitting room,
we laughed so hard, we cried;
poor Sue was doubled up in pain -
I thought she would split her side!

But, I just wouldn't give it up,
no, not by any means;
but the time we laughed the most of all
was when I tried on jeans!

"IF ANYTHING CAN GO WRONG", MURPHY
- vs -
"GIVE UP, 'CAUSE I'VE GOTCHA", O'TOOLE

I used to think that I was nobody's fool
until I met up with a guy named O'Toole.
O'Toole is a step up from Murphy, you see
who brings naught but hardship and trouble to me.

Now you can say fiddle, phooey or pshaw,
but I'm sure you've heard stories about Murphy's law;
Murphy's a novice - this much I know,
compared to Old Murphy, O'Toole is a pro.

O'Toole thinks that Murphy is an optimist,
he finds bringing heartache too good to resist;
while I used to worry about Murphy's law,
now I'm quite sure that O'Toole's the last straw!

TO THE EDITOR

I say words with feeling,
I write them with flourish -
for one simple reason,
my ego to nourish.
I pen words so loving
with the sweetness of honey;
if you care to answer -
please say it with money!

WHAT'S THAT SONG?

It isn't a song by Hamlisch,
or a tune out of Mercer's head;
it's the melody that
my husband snores
while he's lying beside me in bed!

READ THE MANUAL

Instead of saying,
"It's in the manual",
save me the trouble
of thumbing through it;
be kind to me
and simply tell me
what to do
and how to do it!

THIS AND THAT

Now, we have come to the last section
of my book -
writings on a variety of subjects...
seasons of the year,
making a difference in someone's life,
children, pets, retirement,
taking a coffee break,
and one of America's
greatest pastimes... fishing!

CREATIVE AT MIDNIGHT

It seems more often late at night
when I'm getting ready for bed;
an idea for a song or a poem
starts dancing around in my head.

I try to make the thought go away
but, my mind just will not let it;
so, I take the time to see it through,
if I don't I just might forget it.

And though the words that come to me
are way out of my control;
I know when all is said and done,
they are words from my heart and soul!

SEE Y'ALL AT "THE HUT"

There's a place in town that I love to go to
where I'm treated so royally;
and it's not just because the food is great,
it's the faces I love to see.

Whenever the gals see me park my car
and before I enter the door;
they check the coffee immediately -
"Is it fresh? If not, we'll make more!"

They know I like coffee that's fresh and hot
and Tink bought me a special cup;
now each time I walk in, I just hand it to them -
first, they heat it and then fill it up!

I'm always surprised at which server I'll get,
but I must say it never has mattered;
each of them takes such good care of me
and I'm always delighted and flattered!

There's Laurie, Denise, Sunny and Rona,
Jamie, "the twins", and Tammy, too;
Sarah and Tink, and also sweet Becky,
all ready and waiting to take care of you!

I think that this Hut's in a class by itself,
no "if's", no "and's" and no "but's";
yes, the one I go to has just got to be
the best of all Pizza Huts!

Lena Butterworth

a/k/a "The Coffee Lady"

P.S. Okay, the guys are nice, too!

THOUGHTS TO TREASURE

Memories ...

can be treasured in the heart
and quickly brought to mind
to be relived again and again.

Memories ...

can never be erased.

A KIND WORD

Say kind things while I am young
or else I'll have to bite my tongue;
and by the time I'm old and gray,
my tongue will have been bitten away

BLESS OUR GARDEN

Lord, bless our lovely garden
while we are far away;
help it to grow more beautiful
with every passing day.

Lord, see the plants are watered
with rains that gently fall;
and may we soon be here to see
the wonder of it all!

SEWING TIME

There are times when I find myself so in the mood
to sit at my Singer and sew;
but frustration begins when my Singer acts up,
why it happens, I really don't know.

I'm sure that I threaded the needle just right
and everything else seems to work;
so, why all at once does the thread have the nerve
to jam up and drive me berserk?

As my temper gets short and my patience wears thin,
I try it once more and then;
I say to myself not once, but twice,
"Oh, why did I ever begin?"

But the fact that I curse at this sewing machine
isn't the problem, you see;
the problem is that I talk to myself
and find myself answering me!

I LIKE MY COFFEE HOT!

The server fills my coffee cup
and I ask, "Are you sure it's hot?"
"Oh, yes! Of course it is", I am told,
but soon I find that it is not!

I don't know why this happens to me,
how can they be so bold
as to serve me a cup of coffee
that tastes so awful and so cold?

I send it back, then the server brings
a fresh pot and an empty cup;
but when I taste it, it's cold, too,
and I mutter, "I give up!"

I guess it takes a darned miracle
to get coffee that's good and hot;
so I'll wait until I get back home
and brew my own fresh pot!

THE COFFEE BREAK

I've been so rushed today!
I find I've started talking to myself -
"Having a bad day? Need a pick-me-up?"
Okay! It's time for a break anyway.
I've been going at it for hours.
I love to listen to the perking process.
It fills me with anticipation.
Ah! It's ready!
I'll use my good China -
that always makes me feel special.
I'll take a sip, then lean back and savor the flavor.
I'll close my eyes for a moment.
I can hear the birds singing in the trees.
I can feel the gentle breeze -
I love when it brushes against my cheeks.
It's such a lovely day. I hadn't noticed 'til now.
I'll think pleasant thoughts.
Or, I'll not think about anything at all.
Let time stand still.
Whatever needs doing can wait.
Taking time for me is important.
Say! I should do this more often!

LITTLE GIRLS AND LITTLE BOYS

Little girls and little boys,
Oh, Lord! I hate to choose;
it's just so hard for me to make
a choice between pinks and blues.

Girls are pretty and full of fun,
yet so prim and proper in school;
the boys play games with toads and snakes
and break every golden rule.

But a boy is cute and full of life,
just buy him a catcher's mitt;
then toss a baseball into his glove
and watch the big grin he'll get!

Boys are solemn and quiet at times,
but the girls just chatter away;
talking of clothes and boys and songs,
they always have so much to say!

So don't ask me to make a choice,
for that really would be a shame;
I guess when all is said and done,
I love them both the same!

A CHANGE IN COMMUTING

Yesterday I took the train,
today I'll take a cloud;
I'll go where I can dance and sing
and speak my thoughts aloud.

All the worries of the past
I'll quickly leave behind;
and I can set the frames around
the pictures in my mind.

Snug and safe and comfy on
my puffy bed of white;
while twinkling stars protect me
and embrace me through the night.

As the sun awakens me,
I'll slowly rub my eyes;
and marvel as the day unfolds
at every grand surprise.

Never will my heart be sad,
nor lonely will I be;
for there will be such endless joy
and rainbows just for me.

And as my cloud continues on
it's journey quietly;
I'll sail away from mortal view
into eternity.

ODE TO JAKE

I used to think that when I retired
I could sleep 'til the sun came up;
but wouldn't you know, I took leave of my senses
and I got me a little pup.

He whines, he cries and he follows me 'round
like a shadow all over the place;
I try to be firm when I scold him but then,
I look at that cute little face.

When I tell him, "No! No!", he cocks his wee head
'cause he thinks I'm a master who teases;
Yep! One word from me and he goes right ahead
and he does just whatever he pleases.

Yet if I can survive 'til this puppy matures
and keep my head out of the fog;
I'll be able to say with a great deal of pride,
"My goodness! My God! What a dog!"

ODE TO JAKE'S SISTER

I only had Jake for a couple of weeks,
we romped and away time would fritter;
then I brought home a cute female puppy
born in the very same litter.

At first they were friendly, but that didn't last,
for jealousy soon reared its head;
when one turned away from a bowlful of food,
the other one begged to be fed.

Then Jake went from meek to strong macho dog,
but I rained upon his parade;
I rushed to the vet with female in tow,
"Quick, Doc, she has to be spayed!" "Whew!"

If you have intentions of getting two puppies
I'm sorry - I must burst your bubble;
for one puppy surely will keep you a-hoppin',
but two dogs are double trouble!

A TRIP TO THE PET STORE

I asked my love if I could have
one kitten to call my own;
a furry pet to love and care for,
a kitten just mine alone.

So, off we went on a shopping spree,
to "kitty shop", if you please;
but, one can get so awfully confused
with all the kittens one sees.

Then all at once I spotted the one
that touched me through and through;
I whispered so gently in its ear,
"My kitty just must be you!"

Yet, though I stroked its bright shiny fur
while its paws it gently licked;
its sibling almost seemed to say,
"I should be the one that's picked!"

Now, I knew that this was serious stuff,
I didn't know what to do;
my request had been for just one kitten,
how could I dare ask for two?

Still, if I couldn't have them both,
I knew that my heart would break;
how could I separate close-knit kittens -
tell me, how, for goodness sake?

So, I asked my love how he would feel
if someone would tear us apart;
wouldn't we both be lonely and blue
and each have a broken heart?

I pleaded and begged with downcast eyes,
I used all my female charms;
and when we left I had both kittens -
one in each of my arms!

FAITHFUL TO "DYNASTY"

A few nights ago as I readied for bed,
visions of "Dynasty" danced in my head;
Colbys and Carringtons I would soon find,
paraded pompously all through my mind.

With sparkle and glitter from clothing they wore,
pendants and bracelets with diamonds galore;
music that swelled into deep dark of night
and beckoned the dancers 'til first break of light.

And light brought the usual deceitful ploy
of whom to betray and whom to destroy;
Krystle is captive and Dex risks his life,
while a nun is portrayed by Alexis, his wife.

Jeff keeps on searching and now he did find
mysterious Fallon still troubling his mind;
Claudia marries her ex-husband's brother,
how could she bed-hop from one to the other?

146

While Steven's suspicions are foreign to Blake,
Krystle's imposter is quite a good fake;
Sammy Joe plots and connives, to be sure,
alas, my addiction hasn't a cure.

Now more of the Colbys have come into view,
Jason and Sable and three siblings, too;
Constance, Miss Stanwyck, a class act, no doubt,
provides me with pleasure I can't do without.

Shapiros, Spelling and Cramer, please note,
here is my comment and one you may quote;
though faithful to Dynasty, I'll rise above it,
I know it's all trash - but, oh, boy! Do I love it!

THE GUNSLINGER

A gunslinger rode into town one day
with a posse not too far behind;
his rough-whiskered face and his beady-blue eyes
told that he was the murdering kind.

He tied up his horse, then shuffled his steps
through the swinging doors of the saloon;
the tables were full and the music was loud
as the band played a lively old tune.

He dragged his old boots 'cross the dirty floor
and he sashayed right up to the bar;
with parched lips he ordered a straight whiskey drink
and said, "Pardner, I've traveled far."

The bartender watched as the gunslinger reached
and then downed his drink with one swallow;
no one suspected, not for one minute,
the shoot-out that soon was to follow.

The gunslinger shifted his stance once more
and his eyes drifted over the crowd;
then all whispers stopped as the gunslinger moved,
then somebody shouted out loud ...

"The posse's a-comin' - let's all take cover!",
they scattered and hid out of sight;
the thundering hoofs of the posse's swift horses
shattered the still of the night.

The townspeople gathered as gunfire rang out
and the ending began to unfold;
six guns were aimed at the gunslinger now,
but he stood his ground brave and bold.

One bullet sailed through the smoke-filled air,
like a magnet - on target and swift;
a loud thud was heard as the gunslinger fell,
then the gunsmoke began to drift.

A crowd made a circle around the gunslinger,
then one man stepped forward and said;
"All gunslingers, hear, if you come to this town
you, too, will end up stone-cold dead!"

THE DEATH OF HALF A LEGEND

Desi Arnaz died on Tuesday, December 2, 1986, at age 69. If you believe as I do that there is a life hereafter, then Desi Arnaz is not really dead. He has left us to enter the realm of God.

After leaving Cuba and settling in Miami, Florida, he survived by holding a variety of odd jobs. But even then his destiny must have been written in the pages of the future.

Fate brought Desi Arnaz and Lucille Ball together. They were wed in 1940. Each brought into the union of marriage their own special talents, but the combination of those talents was a phenomenon that most of us will not live to see again.

"The Cuban Charmer" and "The Redhead" - the King and Queen of Television, if you please - will ever reign as favorites of the television audience in all parts of the world.

While Lucy kept us in a constant state of side-splitting laughter, the Cuban Charmer was slowly inching his way into our hearts and it is there that he will remain.

A TOAST TO RETIREMENT

To retirement I tip my hat,
for it represents
a little more of "this"
and less of "that" -
and quite a few "no more's".

No more commuter trains to miss -
no frantic deadlines to meet -
no running errands for my "boss"
with hot pavements beneath my feet.

More time to watch the feeding birds -
more time to smell the flowers;
I sit before the cozy fire
and dream away the hours.

No pressure from the long hard days -
tough days that taxed my brain;
no trudging through the mounds of snow -
no more drowning in the rain.

Most certainly I do not miss
the briefs that had to be typed;
no more tomes to be filed in court -
no egos that must be hyped.

Ah! Yes! I drink to golden years,
a time I'll enjoy the most;
I lift my glass to retirement
and heartily drink a toast!

MAKE A DIFFERENCE

Have you made just one person smile today,
or lended a helping hand?
Have you held someone close and whispered softly,
"It's all right, dear, I understand"?

It doesn't take much most times, you know,
to let someone know you care;
just remember the times you needed help,
but you knew someone would be there.

We travel life's journey only one time,
yes, one chance for me and for you;
so, don't make a difference for only one day,
do it every day all the year through!

DO SOMETHING FOR SOMEBODY ELSE

When your problems are many
and joys are too few,
you can bury your head in the sand;
or forget your own troubles
at least for a while
and give somebody else a hand.

You can say you're too busy
and days are too short,
you already have too much to do;
but think of the ones
who can't do for themselves,
so many are counting on you.

Life can be a challenge
and we all have days
when everything's going all wrong;
but try to be helpful
each day of your life,
put priorities where they belong.

Don't let precious time
keep on slipping away,
it's never too late to start;
for when you do something
for somebody else,
what a feeling you get in your heart!

Me - nice stringer of White River Rainbows!

Bill & I enjoying the White River

Son Steve, the happy fisherman!

WHITE RIVER FISHING

A fun day of fishing has just now begun,
I watch as the boats pass by, one by one.
The fishermen truly are one special group;
they're out there in fog thick as hot homemade soup.

In blazing red sun or in downpour of rain,
so avid are they - they all must be insane.
They claim fish bite better whenever rains fall,
but that's justification to be out there at all.

With lines baited up and each cast on the mark,
sometimes they're out there long after dark.
To catch their limit of trout they are wishing,
they're drawn like a magnet to White River fishing.

I've let all their stories fill up my ears
as they stomp and yell and toast with their beers:
"Here's to good fishing - it was a great day,
and we humbly pay tribute to the ones that got away!"

FISHERMEN: A SPECIAL BREED

Living on the White River is exciting! It is not yet daybreak but I can hear the purring of boat motors outside the bedroom window. My eyes try to focus through half-opened lids and finally zero in on the oversized clock numerals across the room. Heavens! The birds aren't even up yet!

I sit on the edge of the bed, my feet moving slowly across the shag carpet in search of soft fuzzy blue slippers. Slippers found, the chill in the room hastens me to close the window.

My body automatically stumbles its way down the hall and around the kitchen island. I stand motionless before the coffeemaker and tell myself, "Yes, dear, it takes water to make coffee."

Cold mornings are such a challenge to this retiree. While employed by a busy law firm in Chicago I could make daily decisions in the wink of an eye. Now I have trouble deciding whether to get the coffeemaker perking, or whether to start a cozy fire to stop my teeth from chattering.

My first sip of freshly-brewed coffee assures me that I have rejoined the human race. I part the draperies at the sliding glass doors and my eyes look furtively up and down the river.

Boats are anchored in a pattern resembling a dot-to-dot puzzle. I've watched people sit in the same spot for a long time having no luck at all. They finally get disgusted and move to another spot. Yet another boat anchors in the same place minutes later and they can't take the fish off their hooks fast enough! Strange sport!

156

Fishermen are a "SPECIAL BREED"! I say this because outwardly they may be robust-looking, timid, extroverted, shy, tall, short and stocky, mild-mannered, or evil-tempered. The same man who becomes impatient while his wife hurries to get ready for a dinner date with "Mr. & Mrs. Boss" has no problem sitting in a boat for hours on end with a worm on his hook.

I've heard the craziest fish stories in my time but the most bizzare was the tale of the fish AND the Polaroid snapshot that got away!

Only two characters are involved in this one-act play -- the fisherman and the good-sized fish he caught. The fisherman set the live fish on the counter near the sink on the dock and placed the snapshot next to the fish.

The fish flipped and flopped. After an aerobatic stunt the fish came down on the edge of the Polaroid snapshot. Both the fish and the picture landed in the river.

When the story was relayed to me later that day I chuckled and said, "Not only do I have to listen to the sad tale of the fish that got away, I have to swallow the fact that the Polaroid snapshot got away, too! That's just too much!"

The biggest "catch" of <u>my</u> life - so far!

SPRINGTIME

The crocus and the lilies
seem to waken from their beds;
they make their way from underground
and show their tiny heads.

And then spring showers soon will come -
it won't be very long -
to nourish them and help them grow
so they'll get big and strong.

I'll say goodbye to winter winds
that made me feel so cold
and just sit back and patiently wait
for springtime to unfold.

BY THE HEARTH

When cold winds blow
I ignore all the clocks
for I have only one strong desire;
and that is to take off my shoes and socks
and wiggle my toes by the fire.

The dishes sit in the sink, if you please,
and the vacuum will stay in the hall;
the laundry can build up clear to my knees
'cause I really don't care at all.

All cuddled up I can watch every flame
as it curls 'round the slow-burning wood;
if this is my weakness I'm not to blame
for it feels so gosh-awful good!

FEED THE BIRDS

High on a limb, a sentry is perched
and the others are all standing by;
they wait and watch and then right on cue,
they all spread their wings and they fly.

Here they all come, my fine-feathered friends,
as they puff up to ward off the cold;
positions are claimed and then they begin
to feast on their treasures of gold.

The bleak winter sky casts shadows of gray
o'er my guests as they eat bits of corn;
colors once bright are all at once dim
and are lost in dense fog of morn.

Then all at once the bright winter sun
shows me clearly their bright-colored heads;
their movements so quick that the colors mesh,
the blues, the yellows and the reds.

At break of day the pleasure I feel
is not easy to put into words;
for no matter what else I do each day,
I remember to feed the birds.

159

AUTUMN'S SONG

Autumn: Fresh! As shiny as a new bicycle;
as brisk as a child's walk;
as beautiful as a Mother's face.

Autumn: Full of surprises and delights;
leaves that come swirling down,
tumbling around, dancing 'round
my head; brown, gold, amber
leaves, falling from the trees
and gliding to the ground.

Autumn: Skies of indescribable beauty,
changing as often as a woman
changes her mind; the crispness
of the morning air that brings a
surge to the blood in my veins and
quickens my pace; the bright sun
covering me like a cozy blanket,
protecting me from the too-soon
awakened wind.

Autumn: Hues breathtaking to the eyes,
invigorating to the soul

Autumn: Magnificent!

GOBLINS AND GHOSTS

The witch rides her broom
as she circles the room
with her black hat and cape,
boy, that's scary!
And a cute little ghost
who really looks almost
like Casper, the friendly,
isn't very!

The screeches and howls
of the old midnight owls
make me shiver and shake
where I'm standing.
Surviving the fright
of a Halloween night
I admit is so very demanding!

But I'm not afraid
of the witches or ghosts,
or black cats,
or goblins and such.
These things never scare me -
no! not at all!
Who, me? Oh, no? Not much!

we give
thanks

A SPECIAL THANKSGIVING

Our Father gave us life,
our country gives us freedom;
freedom to speak our minds
and to worship as we choose.
We have been granted so many
avenues of freedom.
Flanked by our Father
and our country,
we have the right to be
all that we can be.
Through countless battles
and jubilant victories,
each generation has emerged
with a more powerful conviction
and a confirmation that
freedom is the most
cherished privilege on earth -
and it is indeed a privilege.

162

Remember that each of us
has the right to walk proudly.

May we earnestly strive to be
a credit to our country
and, more importantly,
acceptable in the eyes
of our Father.

And, so, a Special Thanksgiving ...

As we gather 'round the table
on this blessed Thanksgiving Day,
we feel the Lord within our hearts
as we bow our heads to pray.

Let us praise and thank our Father
for all the things we hold so dear,
not just on this Thanksgiving Day -
but on every day of the year.

Granddaughter Chris

WHAT IS CHRISTMAS?

Christmas is:
   Christmas trees laden with flickering lights
and glistening ornaments; holiday crowds of bustling
shoppers trying to buy that "last minute" present;
man-made snowmen standing on snow-covered lawns as
if meeting to discuss events of the day.

Christmas is:
   Expressions of anticipation on the faces of
children; the nice feeling of fresh snowflakes melting
on your cheeks.

Christmas is:
   A time for lots of laughter and lots of good times.
Words cannot describe the warm feeling you get at this
time of the year just being with those you love.

Christmas is:
   For children, for Moms and Dads, for Grandmas and
Grandpas and any other relative you could name.

What is the real meaning of Christmas?
   Christmas is a time of joy in remembering the
birth of the Christ Child!

MERRY CHRISTMAS!

May God bless you, children,
may God bless you all
for the fondest of memories
that we can recall.

May God keep you, children,
within His good grace
'til the next time we gaze upon
each smiling face.

May God shine upon you
we hope and we pray;
may you know joy and happiness
this Christmas day.

We still have the closeness
the season imparts;
for the love we share will remain
deep in our hearts.

JOYOUS NOEL

CHRISTMAS! It's a time to say a special prayer giving thanks for our countless blessings, to sing carols and to stand under the mistletoe.

It's a time to build snowmen, go sledding and ice-skating, brush snowflakes from eyelashes, don cozy slippers, wrap presents and trim the Christmas tree.

As Christmas Day draws near, the true feelings of Christmas deepens in each of us. To have those you love, and who love you, near to share any part of this day with you is to truly have God's finest blessing.

THE MEANING OF CHRISTMAS

The wondrous colors of life's majesty ... only seen by those who watch. Christmas colors - red, green and gold.

Christmas! A wonderful time of year! It brings a certain feeling and has a special meaning to each of us in our own way.

Christmas is a time for giving! We sometimes forget that the greatest gifts of all are not material things. A smile, a handshake, a kind word, or a friendly deed without thought of repayment have much more meaning.

Christmas is a time for love! It may mean going out of our way to do something special for someone we care very much about, or it may just mean a special look, without a word, that conveys the feeling we have just being near those we love. Oh, yes! There is plenty of love in the world - only our lines of distribution get clogged.

SANTA CLAUS IS CHRISTMAS

Silver bells and mistletoe
  And a gaily colored wreath;
    Next a tall majestic tree
      The presents underneath.
        A visit, too, from special friends
          Calling to wish you good cheer;
            Lots of memories that will live
              All throughout the year;
                Utterly grand and beautiful, too!
                  Season's greetings to each of you!

This poem was eventually set to music
by my brother, Kelly.

CHRISTMAS IS FOR CHILDREN

Listen children, starry-eyed,
the night is drawing near
when Santa and his magic sleigh
will suddenly appear.
Do not try to stay awake,
my children, but instead,
say your prayers and say goodnight,
then quickly off to bed.
And as you slowly fall asleep
there's magic in the sky;
for Santa goes from house to house,
a twinkle in his eye.
But while you lie there fast asleep,
as sleeping you must be;
Santa's placing lovely gifts
beneath your Christmas tree.
Now how, you ask, can Santa do
the things I say he can?
It's just because dear Santa is
no ordinary man.
So careful what you say, my child,
and careful what you do;
do the things you know you should
for Santa's watching you.
And when you wake on Christmas day,
what wonder and surprise!
There will be such a lovely sight,
you won't believe your eyes!

My brother, Kelly, wrote a
lovely melody to this poem, too.

CHRISTMAS

Christmas is a lovely time,
a special time of the year,
with season's greetings on their way
to loved ones far and near.
Christmas is a sparkling time
of silver and of gold;
a time when you see smiles of joy
on faces young and old.
Trees are trimmed with ornaments
and lights.
My! How they glow!
The presents wrapped so prettily
with ribbons and a bow.
Bound by love on Christmas day
though we are miles apart;
for the holiness of Christmas lies
in each and every heart.

On May 11, 1998 I sent a letter to the editor of our local newspaper in time for the Memorial Day holiday. I enclosed the poem I had written for Bill on March 23, 1995 (see poem on page 38) in the hope that it would be published in time for the holiday. It was not.

Here are excerpts of that letter ...

When my husband, Bill, died on March 1, 1995, I was faced with making all the necessary arrangements for his burial in the family plot in Indiana. Uppermost in my mind was remembering how much Bill loved our country and how proud he was to have served in the United States navy during World War II.

Indeed, he did watch lifelong friends die right before his eyes. I think that's why he never talked much about the war days, but he did mention the time when a typhoon hit his supply ship. He told me that at one point the ship was standing almost on end and that when he was slammed against the deck of the ship face down, the force of his fall broke every tooth in his mouth. He endured agonizing pain and spent weeks in a dentist's chair with never a word of complaint.

I was determined that Bill would receive the full benefit of a military burial on Monday, March 6, 1995. But, two things happened that day that were quite upsetting. The priest who was scheduled to deliver the eulogy never arrived and neither did the representatives of the Indiana VFW. The gun salute did not take place on that day.

After I came home, I couldn't shake the feeling that I had "let Bill down", so I began to make phone calls and write letters. After I had exhausted all avenues locally to no avail, I continued to pray for God's help. He led me to the sweetest man at the VFW in LaPorte, Indiana. Mr. Mike Walt is responsible for making my wish come true, even though more than two months had gone by since the funeral.

At the cemetery on May 24, 1995, I stood alongside Bill's grave wiping the tears from my eyes as I listened to my sister, Luci, read the poem I had written for Bill the night before. Then after a few minutes of silent prayer, the shots fired by the VFW pierced the silence. I thought, "I did it, Bill, I didn't let you down". I made a special phone call to Mr. Walt when I returned home to thank him again for his compassion. He told me he had never attended a more emotional ceremony in all his years. I guess it was because he knew how strongly I felt that if there was any justice in this world, I was not going to give up until I had accomplished what I had set out to do.

Since that day I have basked in the satisfaction of knowing that my perseverance resulted in a well-deserved tribute not only to Bill, but also to the thousands of others who proudly served their country and to the many brave soldiers who perished in its defense.

GOD BLESS AMERICA

I DON'T BELONG TO ANYONE

At this particular stage of my life, I don't belong to anyone. It's just me. When you lose a spouse it can be very lonely and there are times when you find yourself thinking, "How am I ever going to cope?" But, somehow you will and you do.

I must say it's a good thing I like myself because I spend so much time alone these days. There always seems to be a great many daily things for me to do and so keeping busy is never a problem. That's the easy part. The difficulty lies in getting up every day with no one there to wish me a cheery "Good Morning", to give me a hug and a kiss to start my day off on the right foot, to bless me whenever I sneeze, to rub my shoulders and neck after I have spent too many hours at my computer, to scratch an itch strategically impossible for me to reach and, hardest of all, not having someone to gather me up in his arms as we exchange whispers in the dark.

I'm told I'm lucky. I can basically go where I want to go, do what I want to do, buy what I want to buy (within reason, of course), and eat what I want to eat when I want to eat it. But, if I had a choice, I would much prefer to relish precious moments in the arms of a caring, gentle man. Of course, he would have to love music as much as I, continually encourage my writing, enjoy traveling to wondrous parts of our beautiful country and WOW! - if he loves to dance, what a plus that would be!

 174

As for hugs, I love them! Whether it's a bear hug, a "don't-you-worry-things-will-get-better" hug or, the best hug of all, one that means I love you, just bring them on. I'm always ready!

Should you someday find yourself at wit's end, you can take solace in knowing that there are many others somewhere in this world who are experiencing the same situation as you. I have found that the best way to cope is to trust in the Lord because He always knows what's best for you, keep relatives and friends close to your heart and rely on them when necessary and, for heaven's sake, keep a song in your heart and a smile on your face because no one enjoys being around a grouch!

Author's closing thoughts ...

I would enjoy hearing from you after you have finished reading my book. It would please me so much to know how it touched your life. Did you come away with a favorite poem from among those which I have included in my book? Did you enjoy one particular chapter more than the others?

Tell me if my words brought a smile to your face, a ray of sunshine to your day, if you felt a tear or two rolling down your cheeks, or if you enjoyed a chuckle or two and, most of all, if they somehow strengthened your faith. Please send your thoughts and comments to me at P.O. Box 675, Mountain Home, Arkansas 72654-0675. Bless your heart!

We're all in this together, you know. Let's try to love one another - not just say it, but show it as well. Remember that each of us is special in the eyes of the Lord. He feels our pain, He shares our joy and He eases our burdens whenever He can.

Think of it this way: after every night comes daylight giving us another chance to start anew. Every morning say to yourself, "The Lord has given me another day. What a precious gift! What am I going to do with it?" Use it well!

My hope for each of you is that you live life to the fullest in good health for the rest of your days. May the Lord bless you and keep you safe always.

INDEX

INDEX (con't)

INDEX (con't)

To order additional copies of **Words From The Heart**, complete
the information below.

Ship to: (Please print)
        Name _____

        Address _____

        City, State, Zip _____

        Day phone _____

_____ copies of *Words From The Heart* @ $13.95 each $ _____

Postage and handling @ 2.50 per book $ _____

AR residents add 5.625% tax (.79¢ per book) $ _____

Total amount enclosed $ _____

Make checks payable to Lena Butterworth

Send to: Lena Butterworth
P.O. Box 675 • Mtn. Home, AR 72654-0675

To order additional copies of **Words From The Heart**, complete
the information below.

Ship to: (Please print)
        Name _____

        Address _____

        City, State, Zip _____

        Day phone _____

_____ copies of *Words From The Heart* @ $13.95 each $ _____

Postage and handling @ 2.50 per book $ _____

AR residents add 5.625% tax (.79¢ per book) $ _____

Total amount enclosed $ _____

Make checks payable to Lena Butterworth

Send to: Lena Butterworth
P.O. Box 675 • Mtn. Home, AR 72654-0675